EPHEMERA.

Geo. Edward Rice

J. H. Woodward

"Ludere qui nescit, campestribus abstinet armis,
Indoctus-que pilæ disci-ve trochi-ve quiescit,
Ne spissæ risum tollant impunè coronæ:
Qui nescit, versus tamen audet fingere!"

HORACE.

"Now they that like it may; the rest may choose."

GEO. WITHER.

BOSTON:
TICKNOR, REED, AND FIELDS.
MDCCCLII.

STACY AND RICHARDSON, PRINTERS, BOSTON.

PREFACE.

THIS volume of Verse is, by both its Writers, respectfully submitted.

G. E. R.

J. H. W.

Boston, November, 1852.

CONTENTS.

EPHEMERA

EPHEMERA.

ADDRESS TO THE MERMAID.

"Thou comest in such a questionable shape
That I will speak to thee."

HAMLET.

MYSTERIOUS HYBRID! Near the Fejee Isles
  You were entrapped, they say, one Summer's eve,
When, unsuspicious of the seaman's wiles,
  You sweetly sang — but this I can't believe —
With execution that outrivalled GRISI,
Arias from operas by no means easy.

Strange denizen of somewhere in the deep,
  You come to us so very well preserved
That we might think you in the tranquil sleep
  Your innocence and beauty well deserved —
Were not your graceful figure so erect;
And what from Mermaids could we not expect?

But there's no power now in your dark eyes
  To look with scorn upon the dandy's suit, —
You answer not to beauty's smiles and sighs;
  Then must that heart be stilled, that tongue be mute,
And this glass case, excluding you from air,
Proves the sad fact that life is absent there.

I'd promised me a very pleasant task,
  And hoped to pass the evening *tête-à-tête;*
There's many a question that I wished to ask,
  Concerning all the customs of your state, —
I'm getting up a book, and looked to you
For stores of information strange and new.

I wished to know if Mermaids had a king,
  Or chose a president each year or two —
Had stringent laws, — for that's the sort of thing
  To make the populace their duty do; —
Or lived together in a crazed community,
Where each did as he listed, with impunity; —

And all that happens in those coral groves
  We're told you dwell among, far down below;
If you write tender verses to your loves, —
  If there's a place where naughty Mermaids go, —
What time you put the little ones to bed, —
And if they sing such songs as "Uncle Ned."

If you have Mermaid lawyers and divines,
  And if the last say everything is vanity;
Whether you speculate in copper mines, —
  And are not Mermaids subject to insanity;
If pure salt water 's all you have to drink,
And if your tails do n't sometimes get a kink.

Fond of the water you must surely be,
  But do you have regattas every year?
Do you e'er navigate the briny sea
  In sea-weed barks, — or use your tails to steer
Some scooped-out tortoise shells from grot to grot;
And is there any one who owns a yacht?

Are any of the Mermaids politicians? —
  What's their opinion of a certain letter?
Do you not find, if you employ physicians,
  That of their stuff the less you take the better
Your health becomes? In fact, I'm very sure
You must be patrons of the "Water Cure."

Do you prohibit smoking in the streets?
  Do you confine the voting to the males?
What is the salutation when one meets
  Another Mermaid? — Do you shake your tails?
Is charity much practised in the sea, —
Or do you fancy scandal with your tea?

Have you the Magazines and the Reviews?
  Do any of your spinsters have the vapors?
How soon do you obtain the steamers' news?
  And pray, do all the Mermaids take the papers?
Do your young men do military duty, —
And what's the customary price of putty?

But this is useless, — the grim tyrant, Death,
  Has placed his icy hand upon your brow;
Had I been near, to catch your parting breath,
  (It's very safe for me to say so, now,)
I might have got a mass of information
That now is lost to me and to the nation.

I grieve to think some infidels there be
  Who smile in scorn whene'er your name they hear,—
Make it a point to disbelieve in thee, —
  And dare to speak with supercilious sneer,
And say you are a wondrous incongruity —
A specimen of BARNUM's ingenuity.

Shame on that stupid, sacrilegious ass,
Who, thinking no avenger would appear,
Raised from your figure the protecting glass,
And placed a pen behind your well-shaped ear!
And wishing your chaste beauty more to mar,
Thrust 'twixt your parted lips a huge cigar!

'T is difficult my feelings to control,
Whene'er I dwell upon this well-known fact;
The wretch must have an unbelieving soul,—
Would I had caught him in the very act,
I would have brained the dull, unfeeling fool,
Who dared to hold you up to ridicule.

As for myself, I'm willing to believe
In all that travellers delight to tell;
I think the mesmerizers don't deceive,
I frown on those who say that you 're a "sell;"
I think all the magicians superhuman,
And will believe the Giantess a woman.

I place a trust in the Aerial Ship,
My love for the Hydrarchos is quite fervent,—
I 've cruised about our coast to get a peep
At my much slighted friend, the great Sea Serpent;
A man can't put himself to nobler uses
Than taking sides with those the world abuses.

And now, farewell! There 's more that I could say,
For my regard gets every moment stronger,
But I 'll postpone it till some other day,—
This won 't be read if it is any longer,—
You yet shall triumph o'er the sceptic's laugh,
Marvellous specimen of half and half!

A SERENADE.

THE silver orb of night
  Is shining mild above,
A fitting torch to light
  The holy hour of love.
    Then, dearest, wake!
    For o'er the lake
Thy lover flies to meet thee, —
    While to his oar
    The answering shore
Sends echo back to greet thee.

List! how amid the trees
  In heavenly murmur sighs
The love song of the breeze,
  And every leaf replies.

Then, love, let sleep
No longer keep
Those bright eyes from thy lover, —
But lend their light
To glad the night,
Ere night's sweet reign is over.

List! how upon the strand
The rippling wavelets break;
They whisper to the land
The love tale of the lake.
An hour like this
Is made for bliss,
Oh, leave me not forsaken, —
Below, above,
All, all is love,
Then 'waken, love, awaken!

THE CHARCOAL VENDOR.

"Perhaps, and then again perhaps not."
Familiar Saying.

I MEET a fellow often in my way,
  Urging a horse and wagon through the streets,
  And shouting "Charcoal!" to each one he meets;
I came upon him only yesterday,
  But did not feel so much disposed to smile
  At his crocked features and his brimless "tile"
As is my wont; the fact is, I had dined
Extremely well, and felt benign and kind.
  Thought I, "That fellow in those shabby clothes,
Driving all day that shapeless horse and cart,
Owes nothing to the tailor's magic art,
  Like all our gallant, well-dressed city beaux;

And would that all of us, like him, could say
Each night, that our pursuits throughout the day
Had left no tarnish harder to erase
Than what he has upon his hands and face!
There 's not a spot of black upon his heart,
It 's all upon his face and hands and cart, —
And he may stand a better chance to go
To Heaven than I, or many that I know."

But this was Fancy's work, and we,
Though better dressed, perchance, are *just as good as he.*

THE LYRE OF LOVE.

"Θέλω λεγειν Ατρειδας."
ANACREON.

I STRIVE to sing of many a theme,
As o'er the strings my fingers move,
But hushed and silent is the stream
Of music, till my song is Love.

To lay of Sorrow first I struck
The lyre that once breathed music sweet,
Each chord, when touched, that instant broke,—
It would not e'en one note repeat.

Ambition next for theme I chose,
But silent still the lyre remained;
It seemed as if in Death's repose
Each breathless sound and chord was chained.

I'll sing of Friendship, then I said,
  This theme at least will break the charm;
The lyre at Friendship's call was dead, —
  E'en this the spell could not disarm.

Joy! Thou shalt wake my song, I cried, —
  In vain! no melody was there;
The stubborn harp a moment sighed,
  Then ceased, as if in mute despair.

One effort more, — of Love I'll sing,
  Again the tuneless lyre I'll try;
I took the harp, I touched the string,
  Across the wires my fingers fly;

And then in wild, ecstatic fire,
  The music ran the chords along,
I whispered as I kissed the lyre,
  Henceforth I'll sing no other song.

A DOG-GEREL.

SHOWING HOW A CERTAIN STRINGENT REGULATION BECAME REPEALED.

The Councilman to bed had gone,
  Sated with civic glory,
To think upon his mighty deeds
  That still will live in story ;
But scarcely had his eyelids closed,
  And sleep in fetters bound him,
When ghosts of many murdered dogs
  Appeared and danced around him,
      Howling, "O thou Councilman!
      Sanguinary Councilman!
          Corpses we,
          Slain by thee!
      Bloody-minded Councilman!"

The City Father raised his head,
  Waked by this dismal ditty,
And saw the ghosts around his bed —
  The "slaughtered dogs' Committee"—
Hounds, terriers, mastiffs, spaniels, curs, —
  A mangled, motley crew, —
Who yelped and snarled about his ears,
 "We owe our deaths to you!
          O thou Councilman!
          Dog law making Councilman!
              Th' accursed decree
              Was framed by thee!
          Exterminating Councilman!"

The chairman of the ghosts then spoke,
  (A splendid Saint Bernard,
Whom Irish boys had stoned to death,
  In the Eleventh Ward,)
"Of victims to thy law, stern man,
  Here's but a trifling part;

Sent by the murdered crowd, we come
  To mollify your heart.
      O thou Councilman!
      Sapient Common Councilman!
        'T is all thy work,
        Thou barbarous Turk!
      Dog-killing Common Councilman!

"The sands of life for us have run,
  Death's chains will ever bind us,
But we can't rest till something's done
  For those we've left behind us;
The vital spark from us has fled,
  We roam the streets no more,
But every night will visit you,
  Till you repeal the law.
      Come, now, Councilman,
      Be a noble Councilman,
        All scorn defy,
        And remedy
      Your error, Common Councilman."

Then spake that conscience-stricken man,
"I see I've been to blame,
But all the dogs that yet survive
Shall live to bless my name;
The sad effect of what I've done
I view with heartfelt sorrow,
And promise that th' obnoxious law
Shall be repealed to-morrow, —
For I'm a Councilman,
An honest Common Councilman;
'T is my delight
To act upright,
And be an honest Councilman."

Then smiled those ghastly corpses all,
And clapping their fore paws,
Barked out "God bless you! Councilman, —
The city, and its laws;
May you attain, 'mong civic digs.,
The highest of positions."

Then straightway vanished into air
Those canine apparitions,
Singing "Good-bye! Councilman,
Repentant Common Councilman!
Dogs will soon
Change their tune,
And bless the Common Councilman."

WED NOT FOR GOLD.

WOULDST wed for gold? Seek yonder palace-gate,
Where liveried menials at the entrance wait;
They guard the porch 'gainst all of low degree,
But thou, unseen, shalt enter there with me,
And learn a lesson from a gilded page:
Too true the tale it tells, from age to age,
Of wealth and misery joining hand in hand.
See yonder lady fair; wouldst understand
Why on her youthful brow that shadow rests?
Can it be true that aught of grief molests
One who is mistress of a home like this?
What! can not riches purchase earthly bliss?
Fool! list the moral that this scene imparts:
She purchased wealth—with what?—two broken hearts!

Scarce one short year ago, a youthful pair
Plighted their troth, and swore through life to share,
Whether for weal or woe, a mutual lot;
But wealth came limping by, and she forgot
Her faith, his love; alas! poor girl, she sold
His earthly happiness, her Heaven, for gold!
Where is he now, that poor heart-broken boy?
When he beheld his all of earthly joy
Gone, gone for ever with the rich man's bride,—
A tomb-stone tells the mournful tale—"he died."
And is she happy now? No; every scene
She looks upon but tells what might have been.
Though decked in costly silks and satins rare,
Though priceless jewels glitter in her hair,
Though blessed with every thing that wealth can buy,
Still, is she happy? List the stifled sigh
Bursting unbidden from her aching breast!
It sometimes finds a voice, though oft repressed;
And in that sigh a truthful tale is told:
Go, write it on thy heart, then wed for gold!

Wouldst wed for gold? Seek yonder humble cot:
There wealth and misery are alike forgot;
Wide open stands the hospitable door,
And welcome he who enters, rich or poor;
Contentment smiles around with homely grace;
Here jaundiced avarice with saffron face
Would e'en forget his hoards of yellow dust,
And give his millions, could he share the crust
That honest labor renders ever sweet,
(Not always such the luxuries of the great).
See from his daily toil the cotter come:
Full well he knows the loved one waits him home;
Little cares he to share the rich man's part,
His mine of wealth is one true woman's heart;
Like those twin stars that mariners descry
When looking Heavenward in the northern sky,
They seek the Polar Star to track their way
O'er pathless seas, but, lest they wandering stray,
And choose some other orb, the Pointers guide
To it alone, heedless of all beside;

Revolving ever, still they never rove
From out the path that guards the star they love.
So woman's rich affections, pure and true,
Once gained, will ever fondly cling to you,
Though all else change. Let good or ill betide,
Faint not, blest man, an angel 's at thy side !
Constant in death, she whispering points above:
" Dearest, we 'll meet in Heaven, for Heaven is love."
Think well on this, ye fools that seek to gain
A fleeting pleasure for an age of pain !
'T is short-lived pleasure wealth alone can give,
And happier far, methinks, 't would be to live
Poor but contented. Now my tale is told;
Go, write it on thy heart, then wed for gold !

AN ANSWER TO AN INVITATION TO DINE.

———"cui corpus porrigitur."

VIRGIL.

I 'VE just received your invitation
To a rare banquet, thus you yclept it,
And much regret my situation
Is such that I cannot accept it; —
No dining out is there for me now,
I 'm very ill, and that 's the reason;
And could you but look in you 'd see now
That I am laid up for a season.

In payment for my sins I 've caught a
Distressing cold, and am in bed,
With napkins wet with rum and water
Twisted around my aching head.

It seems as if that nameless Gent.,
With cloven foot and sable coat,
On my annihilation bent,
Had fixed his talons in my throat.

My voice, whose tones so deep and pleasant
Have been accustomed to delight you,
Has faded out, and were you present
I could not say what now I write you.
You'll find it not an easy task
Deciphering this wretched scrawl,
But he can some indulgence ask
Who writes in bed against the wall.

So when you read this lucubration,
I must request you 'll not be critical;
Consider that my situation
Is not by any means poetical.
A blister that could draw a wagon
Usurps possession of my chest, —
In dreams I fancy that a dragon
Is breathing fire on my breast.

I'm being now, like gold, refined
With very fierce and raging fires,
But not exactly of the kind
That wit or verse-making inspires.
With not a thing to eat or drink,
One can't be very bright or merry,
I'd feel just twice as well, I think,
If I could have a glass of Sherry.

I'll own the wine cup I have drained
Since I've been stretched here on my back,
But then the wine the cup contained
Is known as Wine of Ipecac;
And that, my candid mind confesses, —
A fact I feel convinced that you know, —
Is not so welcome at one's messes
As that which bears the brand of "Juno."

Just as the clock is striking five
I'll know you're sitting down to dinner,
And at that time, if I'm alive,
I'll pledge you in a draught of Senna;

And sigh to lose those scintillations
  From wit that never yet was spiteful,
And all your brilliant coruscations
  Of fancy that are so delightful.

Please give your guests to understand
  I 'd gladly meet them at that hour,
Were not misfortune's heavy hand
  Upon me with resistless power;
And though "*in propria personâ*"
  To visit them I'll not be able,
My spirit yet may have the honor
  To come and rap upon the table.

When rising from the board the crowd are
  "*Vino cibo-que*" quite "*gravatus*,"
I shall be taking Dover's powder
  And mourning my unhappy "*status*."
Then let me hope you all will think
  Of him who pens this trifling stanza,
And filling up your glasses drink
  Confusion to the Influenza!

LONG AGO.

Dost thou remember, lady fair,
  The willow by the river side?
One eve we sat together there
  Thou promised to become my bride.
But stay, fair lady, speak it not, —
  Thine answer I already know;
Those happy hours are all forgot,
  For it was very long ago.

Dost call to mind the grassy lane,
  All hidden in the little grove, —
Can memory bring it back again?
  'T was there I told thee of my love!

Thy willing hand was clasped in mine,
  Thy lips, — say, did they answer No?
'T is past! and why should I repine, —
  For it was very long ago.

Dost call to mind the trembling kiss
  I pressed upon thy burning cheek?
Hast thou forgot the words of bliss
  Thy sweet and gentle voice did speak?
Nay, lady, do not weep! Thy tears
  Have now no right for me to flow.
I thought to share thy hopes and fears, —
  But it was very long ago.

The willow by the stream is dead,
  The grassy lane, the grove, both gone, —
And thou art to another wed!
  I wander through the world alone,
Yet oft unbidden bursts a sigh,
  And down my cheeks in sorrow flow
The tears I weep for days gone by,
  And memories of long ago.

THE BLOOMER COSTUME.

"The gown? Why, aye; — come, tailor, let us see it.
O mercy, God! — What masking stuff is here?"
TAMING THE SHREW.

Some time ago —
'T is not important any one should know
Exactly to a month, week, day, or minute,
How long ago;
Besides, I do n't like publicly to state
How long I 've been contending against Fate,
Striving for glory that declines to come;
I therefore choose
To use —
Because it notes a number indeterminate —
The word that I commenced with — Some.

Well, then, I 'll say — some time ago,
Not
" Ere heaving bellows learned to blow,"
But
Between that and the present time
Of writing this agreeable rhyme, —
When I was at that tender age
When children are " by Nature's kindly law,
Pleased with a rattle, tickled with a straw."
(See Pope — but I forget the page,)
I used to be delighted to peruse
The immortal melodies of Mother Goose, ·
And never
Imagined anything could be more clever.

The toys and books of childhood are put by,
But different books and toys
Attract the fancy and delight the eye,
When we 're no longer boys.
I 've no idea of giving you a dose
Of sentiment, — but all that I propose

To say,
Is, that I have n't had a look
Into that small aforesaid book
For many a day;
But one sad history
Of Man's atrocity and Woman's wrongs,
Divinely told in one of those sweet songs,
Though left towards the close enwrapped in mystery,
Took such a firm hold of my youthful mind,
(For of such conduct never had I heard,)
That at this moment, were I so inclined,
I could repeat it, word for word,
Though since I read it
'T is now some — Faith, I very nearly said it!

I 'm getting prosy, — that 's a fault of age,
But, my dear reader, do n't get in a rage,
And I will briefly state
The facts, — and if you never read or heard
The story told, will pledge my word
That they 're as I relate.

A market woman, on a market day,
Was, when going home,
By drowsiness quite overcome,
And fell asleep upon the King's highway.
The historian then proceeds to say,
In language most poetical,
That at this juncture critical
"There came by a pedlar, whose name was Stout,
He cut her petticoats all round about,
He cut her petticoats up to her knees,
And left the old woman to shiver and freeze."

That the behavior of the pedlar Stout
Was very wrong, I never had a
Shadow
Of a doubt, —
And presumed that he,
For that dark villany,
Was now atoning, in eternal flame,
(The place of course I should n't dare to name,)

And for ever and ever
Would stay there, and never
With human beings be allowed to mix again ;
But from the exhibitions of this season,
We have good reason
To think that Stout
Has been let out,
And gone to his old tricks again !

A FAREWELL.

Farewell! Farewell! I scarce can bring
  My trembling lips to speak the word;
Its hated accents seem to ring
  Like funeral chimes by mourners heard;
It drags me from the dreamy past, —
  Of buried hopes it tolls the knell,
And happiness retreats aghast
  Before that dreaded word — Farewell!

No more of love, no more of home,
  No more of every joy I prize,
The parting hour at length has come,
  And even friendship withering dies.

No more! What thoughts of deep despair
Those bitter words of anguish tell!
No hope of future resting there,
To light the sadness of Farewell!

Adieu! To thee I will not speak
Of what I fancied once might be, —
'T would bring a blush upon thy cheek,
In pity for my misery.
I will not claim the single tear
Thou couldst not hide, were I to tell
Of what thou needst not, must not, hear, —
'T is whispered in this last Farewell!

Perchance, when ocean rolls between,
Thou 'lt sometimes kindly think of one,
Forgetting what he would have been,—
Remember only he is gone.
Perchance, when all around seems gay,
Thy thoughts may for a moment dwell
On him who can not, dare not, stay,
But bids thee now a last Farewell!

Adieu! adieu! I meant to go
  With placid brow and tearless eye,
Nor deemed 't would wring my spirit so,
  To speak one little word — Good-bye!
I thought to wear a careless smile,
  And with a merry laugh to tell —
Although my heart should break, the while —
  Some idle jest, and then — Farewell!

Yet, fare thee well! I ne'er shall bend
  My knee at morn and eve in prayer,
But supplications shall ascend
  For thee to Heaven, entreating there
That angel hands may round thee twine
  A wreath of happiness, a spell
Of sunny hours, that still may shine,
  Nor ever bid, like me, Farewell!

THE REASON WHY.

HER eye was like the violet,
  When morning dews are on it,
Her cheek outbloomed the damask rose
  She wore in her Spring bonnet;
Her lips like moistened rubies glowed,
  Her hair was chestnut-brown,
Her teeth were like the shining pearls
  That grace a kingly crown.

Her wit was great, her foot was small,
  Her waist was round and slender;
Her voice was low, her figure tall,
  Her heart was very tender, —

And though she was as fair and good
  As Fancy ever drew,
No one proposed! — The fact was this:
  She did not have a *sous!*

"I BRING THEE, LOVE, NO COSTLY GEMS."

I BRING thee, love, no costly gems,
To decorate thy golden hair,
Fresh flowers are Nature's diadems,—
Then let them bloom in fragrance there.

The wave-washed Pearl, from ocean's caves,
The Indian Ruby's roseate dye,
The Diamond, frozen tear of slaves,
Were dim beside thy sparkling eye!

The Opal, rainbow kissed, may lend
Fresh charms to many a form less bright,
But jewels, love, would vainly blend
With thine that ask no borrowed light!

Then take the Rose, whose sunset hue
  Is like the blush upon thy cheek, —
The Heliotrope, whose modest blue
  Seems ever of thine eyes to speak.

The Lily take ; — although thy brow
  Transcends, by far, its snowy white,—
But with the flowers I bring thee now
  Pray decorate thy hair, to-night.

A SMELL OF THE HAWTHORN.

If you 've a philosophic turn of mind,
  I give you joy ! —'t is a delightful thing —
For then you have the will and power to find
  "Sermons in stones, and good in every thing ;"
Therefore, it matters not what situation
You 're placed in, you can find some compensation.

Now I 'm not one who "babbles of green fields,"
  Or for a rural life e'er had a craving, —
There 's not a buttercup the pasture yields
  So pleasant to me as a round stone paving ;
Perhaps my taste 's depraved, — if so, 't is pity,
But I prefer a very crowded city.

'T would have been death to me, some months ago,
  Finding that urgent business summoned me
From this gay town a hundred miles or so,
  Had I possessed not sweet Philosophy, —
For no church penance seems one half so hard
As rustication to a Cockney bard.

What must be, must be! — therefore, like a man,
  I packed my trunk without a single sigh,
(Never to fret, I find the wisest plan,)
  Called not on any one to say Good-bye,
But bought a box of very nice cigars,
And Bulwer's last, and jumped into the cars.

A week passed on, my business was completed,
  And I still lingered, — singular to say, —
With hospitality I was treated;
  Yet 't was not that alone which made me stay,
But at the mansion where I had my quarters
Dwelt one of Mother Eve's most lovely daughters.

Indeed, she was a very handsome girl, —
  Fine eyes, sweet smile, and all that sort of thing;
She had the marble brow, the wavy curl,
  On which the hackney poets' changes ring, —
Perfect she was, as far as outward show went,
But beauty 's not a matter of much moment,

If one is only good, — so people tell us, —
  But yet they always envy its possessor;
And were there shops in town where they could sell us
  Beauty and goodness, there would be a lesser
Crowd 'round the counter where they vended virtue
Than at the other; there the rush might hurt you!

As lodestone attracts steel, or sugar flies,
  Or honeysuckle flowers the brisk bees,
Or candles moths that are not over-wise,
  (Make any other simile you please,)
So Beauty, in all climes and every nation,
Attracts the noble lords of the creation.

But still, although it dazzles and enchains,
  Intoxicates, delights, enthralls, and haunts us,
Want of refinement, or of heart, or brains,
  Or education, quickly disenchants us.
With Helen's self one could not live a day,
If she spelt consolation with a K!

This rustic girl, to whom I've just alluded,
  Attracted me by her uncommon beauty;
And I, my business now quite done, concluded
  To stay a while, — regardless of my duty
At home, — that I might ascertain if she
Had wit and wisdom, and would fancy me.

One lovely evening, — 't was just about
  The termination of the second week, —
(The old folks, bless their souls! had both gone out,)
  I took advantage of the chance to speak
To this sweet Chloe of the woodland wild, —
Dame Nature's unsophisticated child.

I talked of Plato, the divine and wise,—
She merely asked, "Was he a handsome man?"
I told her of the marvels of the skies,—
Sun, moon, and stars, and of their wondrous plan;
And though my explanations were quite clever,
The sole remark she made, was, "Well, I never!"

Did she like Music?... She admired the band
That played when the militia troop came out!
And Poetry?... Yes, when she could understand
(Sweet innocent!) what it was all about!
And Painting?... She much fancied the design
And execution of the tavern sign!

These dampers quite put out what little flame
Her beauty kindled; and I turned away,
Thinking the conversation rather tame,
And promising to see her the next day;
But late that night I took the railway train,
And turned a dweller in the town again.

TO-DAY.

Oh! say not that to-morrow, love,
Is time enough for joy!
The dawn may wake in sorrow, love,
And all our hopes destroy!

The dew-drop seeks the blushing flower,
And greets it with a kiss,
Then perishes the very hour
That consummates its bliss!

Mine be the dew-drop's heavenly joy,
Be mine its happy lot;
E'en if thy kisses, love, destroy,
I'll die, and murmur not.

Love's radiant sun shines bright, to-day,
  To-morrow, clouds may lower;
Then, dearest, let us haste away,
  While yet 't is in our power!

TO A CLASSMATE.

"We have heard the chimes at midnight."
HENRY IV, SECOND PART.

I 'VE long been thinking I should like to hear
Something of one my heart holds ever dear, —
Whether he 's living;
From his deep silence I much feared he 'd gone
Whence there is no return — to that long bourne, —
I 'd my misgiving.

So now, my friend, for want of something better,
I 'll send this very trifling rhyming letter,
To ascertain
If you still live, and recollect the chimes
We 've heard at midnight. Those delightful times
Won't come again!

And how oft-times to Fancy's realms we 'd mount,
And drink deep draughts — from the Pierian fount,
To banish cares;
Then those hot broils — of oysters, down at SNOW'S,
And then the larks — I mean with which we rose,
In time for prayers!

Our class is scattered — some by trade have thriven,
And some have laid their treasure up in Heaven, —
(A safe investment,)
And there are some the young idea who teach,
And some who practice — some who only preach, —
But here 's no jest meant.

Some live in town, their quiet way pursuing,
Who would be pleased to hear what you are doing,
And how you are;
So write us word, in prose, or woo the muse, —
That you do either well, whene'er you choose,
We 're all aware.

How are your talents, — have they run to waste?
Do you still write, — or have you lost your taste
For the poetic?
Are you religious? — Have you joined the church?
And have you found, or are you still in search
Of the æsthetic?

Do you find aught that gives you satisfaction?
Does life present to you the same attraction
It did "lang syne?"
Or have your hopes of winning fame and glory,
And being widely known, in song and story,
Vanished, like mine?

Unless you 've sadly changed, I know you 've gained
That peace that 's purchased by a life unstained,
Upright and moral, —
More satisfactory than vulgar praise,
And better, nobler far, than poets' bays,
Or heroes' laurel.

Write me and tell me how you pass the time,
In your delightful and far-distant clime
Of fruits and flowers.
But ere I close, perhaps you 'd like to know
Of some with whom you passed, a while ago,
Such pleasant hours?

Well; Kate still thrums her tinkling guitar,
And sits and gazes at that favorite star
She named for you, —
And sighs and languishes, and rolls her eye;
She thinks you 're coming back! (At one time I
Believed that true.)

And as for Caroline, she took offence,
Merely because I said she wanted sense! —
So we do n't speak.
Poor little Sue, with whom you used to ride,
Last June fell ill, turned pious, and then died! —
All in a week.

How could you find it in your heart to leave her!
She was a splendid girl; in fact, I never
Have seen a finer.
Her sister Jane—whom, doubtless, you remember—
Married a Missionary, last November,
And went to China.

And now, farewell!—my horse is at the door;
I'm for a ride, and therefore can't say more.
I really miss you,
And mean to write again, some future day,
But now I've merely time enough to say
God bless you!

FALSE CHARITY.

Aye! give your thousands in an idle cause,
Break through your fathers' and your country's laws,
Forget the precepts once so dearly prized,
Be all your former principles despised!
But while ye drain your hoards for other lands
Can ye be blind to what your own demands?
Can ye o'erlook the many suffering poor
Who beg their daily bread from door to door?
Pleading the task of aiding foreign slaves,
Deny to them the mite their hunger craves!
Bestowing millions on some project wild,
Refuse a penny to a famished child!
All this ye do, vain fools! — all this, and more!
And is it Charity that claims your store?

Ask yourselves this; draw back the misty veil
That hides your hearts,—let conscience tell the tale.
Does aught of charity the gold supply?
What, no response! Wilt give me no reply?
Then I will answer truly, for ye all:
'T is Pride!—the sin that caused an angel's fall!
'T is Pride!—that hurled a holy spirit down
From highest Heaven, and caused a God to frown
On those He loved the dearest, best, before!
Oh, search your hearts, and gather from your store
At least the crumbs, and give them to the poor.
'T was but an hour ago I saw a form,
That dragged scarce half a body through the storm,
'Twixt bending crutches, slowly on his way,
From closing door and closing door, to pray
A little aid, to save his only son;
And unassisted, still he tottered on.
I know not if 't was pity bade me speak,—
I could not help it, for he looked so weak,
Methought that every step would be his last;
He seemed to stagger in the wintry blast

As if he had not strength to hold him up.
Poor man! he must have drained the bitter cup
Of pain and penury e'en to the dregs! —
And now — the hardest pang of all — he begs
From men of wealth a mite, to save his boy, —
Not for himself, — no! sooner far destroy
His hated life, and end at once his woe;
But for his child he will descend so low,
And cringe to avarice, can he only save
His chiefest joy and blessing from the grave.
List to the tale he tells! — Columbians, hear!
And for the love of all you hold most dear,
Forget it not. — Remember those at home.
First give to these, then let your pity roam
O'er all the world; — chief in your hearts should be
Your country's claims, — not those beyond the sea!
"Six years ago went up a mighty cry,
From North and South, of War and Liberty.
With many thousands more I took the field,
Resolved to die or conquer, ne'er to yield;
In many a battle willingly I shed
My blood, like rain. A brother left I dead,

On Cerro Gordo's sanguinary plain;
At Cherubusco's fight I stood again,
Close by another; he, too, dying, fell
E'en at my feet! O God! I loved him well! —
Yet on, still on, I pressed, till — harder lot —
I too, fell — wounded by a cruel shot; —
A helpless, useless, broken-hearted man,
At last I gained my home." Hear this who can,
And check the blood that mantles o'er your brow:
His grateful country has forgot him now, —
His withered laurel has to cypress turned; —
From ev'ry door the wounded man is spurned,
While eager hands throw down the heaps of gold
Before a self-made idol, — as of old,
When Israel at Jehovah dared to laugh,
And gave their wealth to build a molten calf.
But list the tale: "I gained my native land,
Maimed, and in want. Of all that stalwart band
Who, but a year before, went forth in pride,
But few remained, — the greater part had died
Of fell disease; or, on the battle-field,
Face to the foe. Columbia's fame was sealed

And signed in blood! Wives, parents, children, mourn
Loved ones departed, never to return!
Full many a widow welcomed us with tears;
Our grateful country welcomed us with cheers, —
Then gave us — to requite the blood we shed —
Medals! — which we were forced to sell for bread!
Aye! sell for bread; no other means remained,
To stay our hunger. — Medals, bravely gained,
For food and raiment!" God, in whom I trust,
Are such things true? Can it be right or just
To aid each useless and chimeric scheme
With wasted thousands? Strive to fill a stream
With drops of water till it flood its banks,
Repay a friend's devotedness with thanks;
Attempt to curb a whirlwind with thine arm;
Preach love to tigers, silence to the storm,
When these ye do, 'tis time enough to free
The shackled nations by thy charity.
Begin at home — there's many an object here
Has claims upon thy bounty, far more near
Than those ye aid so freely, far more dear

To every honest, patriotic heart,—
Claims that are pressed with no rhetoric art,
But plead in withered frames, and sunken eyes!
Delay no longer, lest another dies
Ere ye resolve. Haste, haste, the hours fly fast!
Though late, determine to be just, at last.

PULCHERRIMA.

THOUGH from my boyhood I have felt
A love for Beauty, and have knelt
    And worshipped at her shrine,
Yet never have I known, 'till now,
While gazing on that lovely brow,
    And those dear eyes of thine,
The might of the enchanting spell
Of which the poets often tell.
Yes, lady fair, until this hour
I knew not Beauty's magic power!

THE TEARS OF THE VINE.

The day is done,
The setting sun
Has faded in the West;
The stars of night
Are shining bright,
The birds have gone to rest.
Then brothers dear,
Come gather here, —
Each anxious thought resign,
We 'll drown all care,
And drink the fair,
In the sparkling tears of the vine.

We 'll banish gloom
Till morning come,
Though clouds of sorrow lower;
Your goblet fill,
And every ill
Shall own its magic power.
This night shall glee
Triumphant be,
And rosy wreaths entwine,
To crown the bowl,
And glad the soul,
In the sparkling tears of the vine.

'Till death draws near
We 'll gather here,
And quaff the cup of gladness;
Though fortune frown,
In wine we 'll drown
Ere breathed, the sigh of sadness;

And when at length,
With fading strength,
Our life we must resign,
To mem'ries past
We 'll drink our last,
In the sparkling tears of the vine.

A BENEFICIAL NAP.

"Ne'er was dream
So like a waking."

WINTER'S TALE.

LAST night I sat alone, before the fire,
And watched the coals grow ashy and expire.
So fade away my youthful hopes, said I, —
When instantly I heard a low, deep sigh; —
  I started; and from out the fire-place
I saw a shadowy, sylph-like figure rise,
  That stepping forth, unveiled a lovely face,
And turned on me a pair of brilliant eyes.
"Behold, and listen, but speak not!" said she;
"For once disclosed thy Guardian Angel see!
Where'er you go, whether you walk or ride,
I, though unseen, am ever by your side.

Why this despondency? With pain I see
This fainting heart, and lack of energy;
Do not despair. If not to you belong
The God-like mind, the heavenly gift of song,
Still much can yet be done; you have your part
To play on Life's great stage: be of good heart;
Much is required from every one of those
To whom is given much. Of joys and woes,
Of pain and pleasure, nearly an equal share
Is given to each; — all have some load to bear,
Thine by no means the heaviest. You might see,
Could you read hearts, that many envy thee.
Do n't magnify each petty, trifling ill, —
'T will pass away. Have a determined will;
Press on, and falter not! — The still, small voice
Of Conscience will approve, and cry, Rejoice!
At every triumph; be by that sustained.
Act well the part for which you 've been ordained.
I 'm not the only one to whom you 're dear, —
There 's many a friend who 's watching your career,

To whom, years hence, 't will give delight to say
You tired not, nor halted on your way.
"Be just, and fear not;" to yourself be true,
All will be well. Adieu! my friend, adieu!"

I looked around; — my lights were burning low —
I must have been asleep. 'T was even so.
A good long hour had I been sitting there,
In Morpheus' arms, though in my easy chair.
But Hope had risen, — I felt quite delighted,
Convinced that all Life's flowers were not blighted;
And though of wealth I'd not a sovereign more
Than when I fell asleep, an hour before,
Still I'd gained something — a contented mind,
That for sometime I'd tried in vain to find,
And I resolved that, whatsoe'er my fate,
I yet would "learn to labor and to wait."

SPRING TIME.

SPRING time is coming, all laden with flowers,
Spreading her mantle of green o'er the bowers.
The Lark, high in air, is beginning to sing
Her song of rejoicing, to welcome the Spring.
Brooks are flowing,
Life bestowing,
Lovely Nature seems to fling
All her charms,
With willing arms,
In the lap of blooming Spring.

Silver-haired Winter before her is flying,
In the depths of the valley unwept he is dying,—
Save the tears of compassion that pity may wring
From the bright eyes of April — the infant of Spring.
Birds are mating,
Bliss relating,
In each tuneful strain they sing;
Haste! then, dearest,
Love seems nearest,
Holiest, brightest, in the Spring.

TO SYLVIA.

I KNOW my heart 's no longer mine,
By many an unerring sign;
The blush that mantles o'er my cheek,
When others of thee chance to speak,—
The quickening pulse, the sudden start,
That sends the life-blood to my heart,
And thrills my inmost soul, whene'er
Thy footstep or thy voice I hear,
And vanishes when by thy side
All my philosophy and pride.

Time cannot from my heart erase
The impress of thy lovely face;
And stern indeed is the decree
That bids me to hope naught from thee!
As mariners regard the star
That beams upon them from afar,
And designates their proper way,
When, compass lost, they've gone astray, —
Or as idolaters the sun —
To be adored, but not be won, —
So must I learn to think of thee,
How hard soe'er the task may be;
And though I would that I might claim
To call thee by a dearer name
Than friend, — that seems by far too cold, —
But Fate, that cannot be controlled,
Has interposed; I'll not regret
That thou and I have ever met, —
But while the light of life shall last,
Will think of happy moments past,

Ere from that pleasing dream of thee
I woke to the reality.
But fare thee well!—through life thou'lt move,
Encircled, not enthralled, by love,
And at thy feet, enchanting maid,
Heart after heart will still be laid,—
But none that's offered at thy shrine
Can beat for thee as true as mine.

THE FORSAKEN.

I FEEL no more thy cruel art,
  And bid adieu with tearless eye,
I cannot free again my heart,
  But I can let it break and die.
Perchance I e'en shall strive to smile,
  When thou art to another wed,
But I implore thee, wait awhile,
  Nor claim thy bride 'till I am dead.

I thought not thus the dream would end,
  Oh, 't was a hard and bitter waking!
But cease thy falseness to defend,
  Go and forget the heart now breaking.

The evening sun may rise to-morrow,
The parting ship return to shore,
But all my hopes have set in sorrow,
Have set to rise again no more.

TO AN EDITOR.

I DON'T know why it is, sometimes
   (Perhaps it is the weather,)
I find the knack of making rhymes
   Has left me altogether;
And e'en a draught of Schreider's wine
Can 't give me strength to write a line.

'T is so to-day; for half an hour,
   This rainy afternoon,
I 've tried, but find I 've not the power
   To start a single tune;
The wingéd horse, on some account,
Is not inclined to let me mount.

Of my ideas I'll clothe the whole
  In verse, some future time,
But now, to save my precious soul,
  I could not coin a rhyme;
And as you know my warm regard,
Presume you will not take it hard.

None of your Poets have, of late,
  Made calls upon their muse,
I trust they've met with no sad fate,—
  Perhaps they've got the blues;
If so, a trot upon the road
Would do them all a "power of good."

There's nothing, when one's very blue,
  (And who sometimes is not?)
To make him feel "as good as new,"
  Like a smart, rattling trot!
I found that out, sometime ago,
And try it oft, and ought to know.

When you 're beneath a clear, blue sky,
  And on a noble horse,
The "*vivida vis animi*"
  Returns at once, of course.
When Pegasus disdains the strings,
Just try a nag that has no wings.

The clouds begin to break away,
  And show a patch of blue,
And now the sun shoots forth a ray,
  So pen and ink, adieu! —
I 'm for the saddle, — but to-night,
When I return, I 'll surely write.

"I SAW HER FIRST AMID A THRONG."

I SAW her first amid a throng
  Of gallants brave and ladies fair,
Her's was the gayest, happiest song,—
  She was the brightest being there.

A happy smile played 'round her mouth,
  Like sunshine on a placid lake
When zephyrs from the sunny South
  The golden-dimpled ripples wake.

I scarcely dared to ask the name
  Of her who seemed so fair and bright,
Yet to my brow the heart-blood came,
  As near me oft she passed that night.

We met again, and I had known
  On life's dark ocean many a storm,
Full many a year had swiftly flown, —
  Alas! how changed that angel form!

The hand of Death was on her brow,
  So low her voice she scarce could speak;
Her hazel eye was sunken now,
  And pallid the once rosy cheek, —

Save where a deep carnation flush
  Was shining on the snowy white;
I knew it was a flower whose blush
  Foretold the quickly coming night.

'Twas on the rolling deep we met,
  She sought for health a sunnier shore,
But ere the second sun had set,
  Her pilgrimage of life was o'er.

Yet still that happy smile was there;
  Cold, heartless Death forgot his power,
And pitying, resolved to spare
  The beauty of the withered flower.

Poor girl! alas, no tree shall wave
  Its drooping branches o'er thy head,
For wide and fathomless the grave
  Where thou wast calmly, sadly laid.

No love-sown flower e'er shall bloom
  Above the spot where thou dost sleep,
No sculptured stone shall mark thy tomb,
  For friends to wander there and weep.

Yet many a heart enshrines thee still,
  And many a thought and tear are given,
While hopes, rich hopes, each bosom fill,
  To meet thy angel soul in Heaven.

TO ———.

THE breeze is fair,
The fading land will soon be gone,
And o'er the deep I bear
A heart that thinks of thee alone!

Thy voice so sweet,
Seems whispering to my listening ear;
I turn thy smile to meet
And find 't is but the wind I hear.

Thy gentle face
And figure, that so sylph-like seems,
With its supernal grace,
I may not see, except in dreams.

While life remains,
Thy image ne'er shall leave my heart;
And when in dying pains
I'm forced from all on earth to part,

Then through the air
My soul released shall soar above,
And bear aloft a prayer
For thee and all whom thou may'st love.

"NEVER DESPAIR."

Never despair! Press ahead on thy way,
Fear not though the clouds lower darkling to-day,
Fear not though thy heart is encurtained in gloom,
Press onward! To-morrow the sunshine may come.
The day-star is there and ere long 'twill be shining,
The Heavens are blue, then away with repining.
The pathway before thee, though steep, is still open,
Press on! though the road may be rugged and broken,
Think not of thy former misfortunes with sorrow,
Resolve to retrieve them to-day and to-morrow.
Though friends may forsake thee, the cold world be
frowning,
Press on! and success shall thy efforts be crowning.
You ne'er can replenish a light purse with grieving,
Then let a light heart be the balance relieving,

'T will weigh down the purse and e'en make you forget it,
'T will fill it, perchance, if you only will let it.
A heart that is light is a true golden treasure,
For it joys in itself, nor looks elsewhere for pleasure.
'T is a sun ever shining on all who are near it;
'T is a sweet playing lute to whoever may hear it;
'T is a mirror reflecting all others in gladness;
'T is a curtain to hang o'er the dark brow of sadness;
A diamond that shines, though surrounded in gloom;
A lamp to illumine the mists of the tomb.
Never despair! Life yet is remaining,
To give thee fresh chance of the vict'ry obtaining.
Far, far in the distance hope beckons thee on,
Think not of the idle days faded and gone.
Press on! for the sun in thy sky soon may set,
Then waste not the moments in useless regret;
No time now is left to reflect on lost chances,
Thy life every hour to its ending advances.
Let all thy transactions be honest and fair,
And e'en let thy watchword be, "Never Despair!"

ROMEO MONTAGUE TO JULIET CAPULET.

DEAR JULIET, come down from your lattice so high,
  I've no ladder with which I can reach you;
There's no dew on the grass and the walks are quite dry,
  Then, dearest, descend, I beseech you!
Love making you'll find very nice, if you'll try,
  And I'm just the person to teach you.

I've come over roads very stony and rough,
  And through perils severe that beset me,
Nor tarried to ask of each Capulet gruff
  If to love you he's willing to let me;
I think I'd have given a dose "*quantum suff.*"
  To all of them, if they had met me.

At a very great risk to my clothes and my neck,
I have clambered right over the wall,
And the broken glass bottles its summit that deck
Did not scare or restrain me at all, —
Though I knew I should be a most terrible wreck,
If by chance I had happened to fall.

Nor fear I the sword of your big, burly brother,
Who, perhaps now is hovering nigh,
But I'll dare every danger each night for another
Bright glance from your dark rolling eye.
It's no easy thing, let me tell you, to smother
The flame that is lighted on high!

He who's never been wounded may well jest at scars,
And to overcome peril essay,
Broken bottles set endwise, nor locks, bolts, and bars,
Can keep a true lover away;
Then by the soft light of the innocent stars,
List to all the sweet things I've to say.

But what you complain of it seems is my name,—
I would I'd my visiting card,—
For although for my cognomen I'm not to blame,
Yet I swear I would tear up the word;
But for such a slight cause to extinguish love's flame
Would truly be vastly absurd!

The flower that long since was christened a rose
Would assuredly seem just as sweet,
And be as agreeable to one's eyes and nose,
If we called it a carrot, or beet,—
And I, as John Smith or Tom Brown, I suppose,
Would appear just as well in the street!

So, in order no more to be under a ban,
And denied an access to your door,
I'll have my name altered as soon as I can,
Nor be Romeo Montague more;
To think aught a sacrifice, I'm not the man,
That is done for the girl I adore.

Then, Juliet, descend from that balcony high,
  I've a sermon on Love that I'll preach you,—
We'll take a nice walk 'round the garden so dry,—
  So, dearest, come down, I beseech you;
Love making you'll like, if you'll only once try,
  And I know 't will be pleasant to teach you!

MAID OF THE SOUTH.

MAID of the South! 'neath the moon's gentle light
I am pacing the deck, on this beautiful night;
My swift bark is speeding its course o'er the sea,
And, Maid of the South, I am thinking of thee!

Maid of the South! thy sweet music I hear,
For memory repeats every note to my ear;
Every wave as it breaks seems to whisper to me,
And, Maid of the South, they are whispering of thee!

Maid of the South! thou art sleeping, I know,
For the night is far spent and the moon's sinking low;
Art thou dreaming of one who is out on the sea?
Sweet Maid of the South, art thou dreaming of me?

Maid of the South! Night's pale crescent has set,—
And I saw its last ray with a tear of regret,
For it told of sad parting and absence to me,
Yet Maid of the South, I'm still thinking of thee!

TO THE CITY OF COLOGNE.

"You are smelt
Above the moon."

CORIOLANUS.

I HAVE travelled, by land and by sea,
Many leagues, since to manhood I've grown,
But ne'er, until now, did I place
My nose in thy city — Cologne!

Not the spicy Arabian perfumes
Are the only perfumes I have known,
But I never before was assailed
By such a vile odor — Cologne!

A man in this part of the world
  Should n't be over nice, I will own,
But my system, I fear, wo n't endure
  A long stay in this odor — Cologne.

I have heard of the real Farinas, —
  I believe there 's a thousand and one, —
And now I 've discovered the reason
  Why they make so much Eau-de-Cologne.

My purse do n't increase in its weight,
  The longer from home I am gone,
But I felt quite delighted to find
  I could pay what I owed here — Cologne,

And have enough left me to charter,
  If need be, a steamboat alone, —
For, cost what it might, I 'd resolved
  To get far from thy odor — Cologne.

I trust my olfactory nerves
Will regain soon their natural tone,
But it seems now as if they could ne'er
Smell aught but thy odor — Cologne!

There are some things one cannot forget,
Unless Mem'ry gets knocked off her throne,
And I'm sure I'll remember till then
Thy most villainous odor — Cologne!

So, with joy I now bid thee farewell! —
And from here all the way up to Bonn,
Between every whiff of my pipe,
I'll be smelling thy Eau-de- / odor — } Cologne!

THE BLIND BOY TO HIS BROTHER IN CHURCH.

I AM not blind, dear Brother, now,
For though I cannot see —
Though darkness overspreads my brow —
The Gospel shines for me.

List! Brother, list! each holy word
Is graven on my mind;
I could not see, but then I heard, —
Brother, I am not blind!

Father! to whom all suppliants kneel,
I ask not worldly sight;
Oh, hear a poor blind boy's appeal
For more of Heavenly light!

STANZAS.

> "Give me a bowl of wine;
> I have not that alacrity of spirit
> Nor cheer of mind that I was wont to have."
>
> RICHARD THE THIRD.

'T IS evening, and each star above
  Right brilliantly doth shine, —
And to the health of her I love
  I drink this Margaux Wine.

A thousand leagues my heart returns
  To lands beyond the brine, —
To her for whom my spirit yearns,
  To whom I drink this Wine.

Her figure, graceful as the fawn,
  And slender as the vine
From which the clustering grapes were torn,
  To make this glorious Wine,

Would gain new strength could she but print
  Her foot beside the Rhine;
And her pale cheek would wear a tint
  As rich as Margaux Wine.

The moon would have a softer charm,
  A light still more divine,
If she were leaning on my arm —
  To whom I drink this Wine.

If there is virtue in a prayer
  That flows from lips of mine,
She shall be kept from grief and care,
  And pure as Margaux Wine.

For her the Angels in the skies
  Shall all their powers combine,
And naught shall dim her beauteous eyes,
  Now bright as Margaux Wine.

NOTE. The "Printers' Devil" inquires if Margaux Wine is made on the Rhine; and upon being replied to in the negative, ventures to suggest that it would seem that it was, from the foregoing verses. The writer thinks not; but as celestial wisdom sometimes falls from the lips of babes and sucklings, so perhaps a sagacious criticism has issued from the mouth of this little imp of darkness.

THE FUTURE.

THE dim and shadowy Future! — who can say
What is the Future? Not one single day
Canst thou, O mortal, scan the great "To Come!"
We know the grave must be our final home
Upon this earth, and that is all we know;
Along the past we look — as, o'er the snow
The weary traveller, turning, views each mark
His foot has made distinct; — but through the dark
Unknown Futurity, thou canst not peer.
Believe! Make Hope thy guide, and let her cheer
Thy onward way; look upward to thy GOD,
Nor strive to look beyond! — And when the sod
Covers the clay that now confines thy soul,
His hand shall guide thee to the wished-for goal!

Trust thou in Him, and learn thou from the Past
To shun the snares that sin would 'round thee cast;
Make of thy former life a well-read book, —
Inscribe it on thy heart, that thou mayst look
Upon its page whene'er thy footsteps stray;
Make it a finger-post to point the way
That thou must follow! — Read the Past aright, —
'T will be a beacon in the darkest night,
To light the narrow path that thou shouldst tread;
The Past is for the living, not the dead!

See yonder monument that towers on high!
'T is not alone to tell the passer by
Some patriot, sage, or hero, lies beneath,
For whom 't was raised. And for the laurel wreath
What cares the dead? He cannot see it now;
He cannot wear upon his worm-seared brow
The marble chaplet that is chiselled here
Upon the stone; or feel the grateful tear
We drop upon the flower that blossoms o'er
His lifeless form. His boat is launched from shore

Upon that fathomless and unknown sea —
The boundless ocean of Eternity!
Come; read with me the epitaph, — 't will speak
Volumes of richest teachings. Let us seek
To know the reason why such costly pile
Tells of the dead. What! Cynic, dost thou smile —
As if the grave-yard could no lesson tell
To such as thee? — Go thou, and read it well;
Carve every epitaph upon thy heart,
'T will make thee happier, wiser, than thou art.
Read this: "He was a good and honest man;"
Read, aye, and emulate him, if you can, —
"He loved his country, and for her he died."
Is there no lesson here? See, far and wide,
Your country torn by faction, and for what?
Oh! have ye all so speedily forgot
The sea of holy blood your Fathers' shed?
Tear down your monuments, disentomb your dead,
Scatter their ashes to the winds of Heaven!
Revile their names, and ye may be forgiven,—

But, the great Fabric they erected, spare!
Forbear! — deluded Fools! In time, forbear!
Once severed, ye can never more unite
The glorious chain your Fathers' forged so bright!
Break but one link and every hope is gone, —
Not even the strongest State can stand alone!
What! shall our flag — the banner of the free —
Be furled forever o'er the boundless sea!
And wave no more in glory o'er the land?
Say, would ye on your Fathers' memory brand
The damning tale that they so long have fought,
Through long, long years, and bled and died for naught?
Would'st rend asunder every well-known stripe! —
Blot out each star? Vile Traitors! would ye wipe
From off the book of Nations what has been,—
The noblest page that book has ever seen,—
And give one only stripe to every State —
One only star? Pause, ere it be too late!
Think what ye do! Look backward o'er the Past, —
Read there thy country's welfare, — bind her fast

In loving bonds of Union! let the sun
Of Liberty its course of glory run.
Columbia! — My loved country, rise again
From thy debasement! Wash away the stain
That sullies the bright radiance of thy face!
Cursed be thy sons that would their land disgrace!
Still may thy glorious standard float unfurled,
Ever the pride and glory of the World!

TO A BUTTERFLY AT SEA.

Now, really, it seems kind, though queer,
That you should call to see me here!
        But I'll address you;
And though I cannot understand
How you got out so far from land, —
And you can't tell, — yet there's my hand, —
        I greet and bless you! —

But should as soon expect to see
Moss-rose buds on the main-crosstree;
        (Ah! how I'd pet them!)
Or 'round about the capstan's foot
A bed of violets taking root,
And telling me, although they're mute,
        Not to forget them! —

Or 'neath the shadow of the sail
A lily rearing up her pale
    And lovely face,—
As on the ratlines to espy
A gay and brilliant butterfly,
Seeking in vain, with anxious eye,
    One flowery place.

'T is so; but if you've no objection
To stay, rely on my protection;—
    For you're to me
Suggestive of green fields and flowers,
Woodbine and honeysuckle bowers,
And call to mind delightful hours,—
Of which, when sadness overpowers,
    I think at sea.

The pantry door shall ne'er be closed,
And not a wish shall be opposed,
    If you'll remain.

The sugar-bowl shall yield its sweets,
We 'll give you some luxurious treats,
And ope our many potted meats,
    And best champagne.

Go, range the cabin through and through,
And trust me when I swear to you, —
    As I 'm a sinner, —
That should the steward thwart thy wishes,
I 'll break his head with his own dishes,
And hurl his carcass to the fishes,
    For dinner.

You heed me not! — and now you 're gone,
To tempt the mighty deep alone
    And unprotected.
No! One who hears the raven's cry,
And marks each sparrow fall and die,
Watches o'er all, with sleepless eye, —
And even a simple butterfly
    Is not neglected.

And he the rhymester, who to-day
Has wooed you in an idle lay,
Is but like you—
A wanderer across the seas,—
And dreams away these days of ease,
Entranced with idle fantasies,
Sweet, though untrue.

And though to serious contemplation,
And calm and pious meditation,
Too oft a stranger,
Knows that the strong, protecting arm
That can subdue the fiercest storm,
Is thrown around his powerless form,
In time of danger.

THE END.

www.ingramcontent.com/pod-product-compliance
Lightning Source LLC
LaVergne TN
LVHW021426110826
845150LV00007B/2110

* 9 7 8 1 4 2 5 5 0 7 5 7 2 *